Fantastic Dinosaur Facts

by Leonie Bennett

Consultant: Dougal Dixon

CONTENTS

Words in **bold** are explained in the glossary.

The biggest dinosaur

Look at Supersaurus.
It was probably the biggest
dinosaur ever.

It was as heavy as 50 elephants.

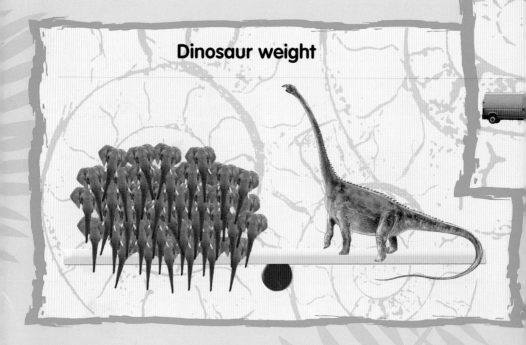

Dinosaur weight

It grew to 40 metres long. That's longer than eight vans.

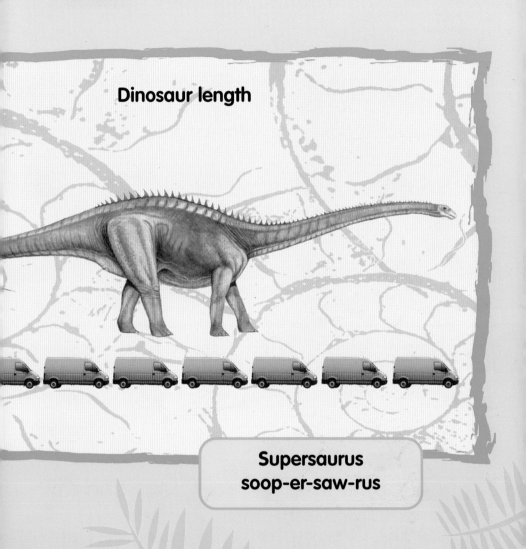

Dinosaur length

Supersaurus
soop-er-saw-rus

The smallest dinosaur

Look at Microraptor.

It was probably the smallest dinosaur.

Dinosaur size

It was as small as a chicken.

It had feathers on its arms, legs and tail.

It had long claws. It used its claws to hold on to trees.

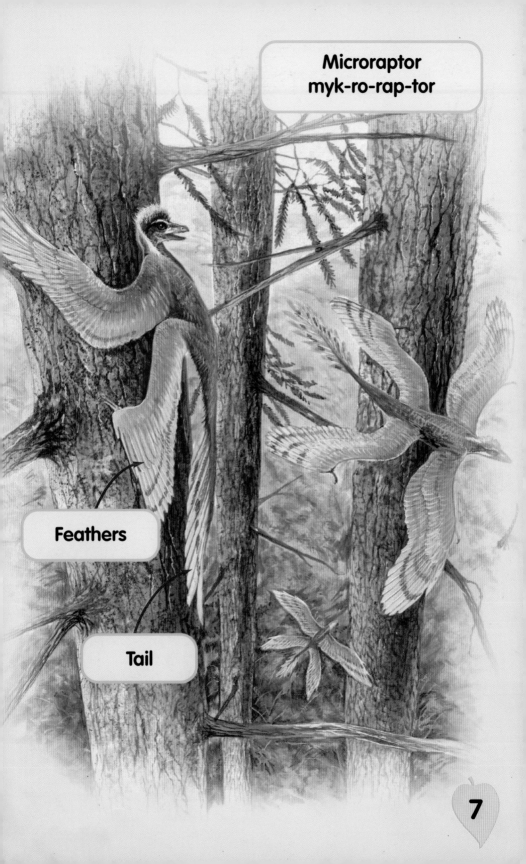

Microraptor
myk-ro-rap-tor

Feathers

Tail

7

Big head

This was probably the biggest **meat-eating dinosaur**.

Giganotosaurus
jie-gan-ot-o-sor-us

It was bigger than T. rex.

This dinosaur's head was as big as a leopard.

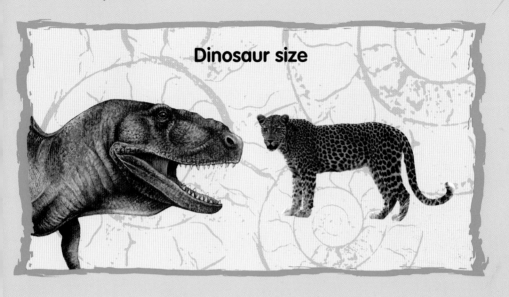

Dinosaur size

Some of its teeth were 15 centimetres long.

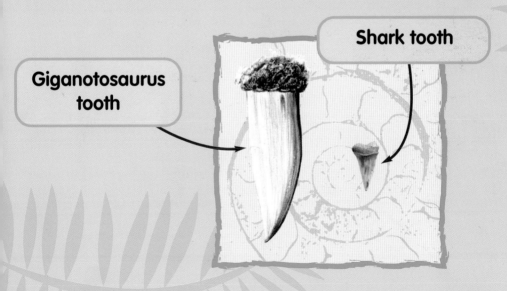

Shark tooth

Giganotosaurus tooth

Big brain

Troodon was a small dinosaur but it had a big brain. It was probably the smartest dinosaur.

It had big eyes to hunt its food at night.

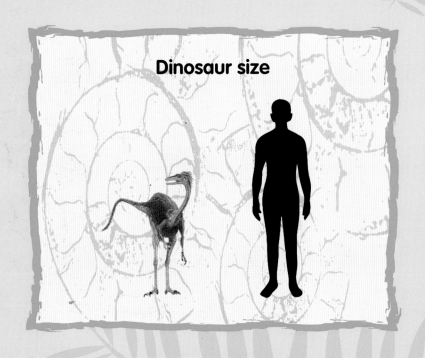

Dinosaur size

Troodon
troo-o-don

Eye

11

Keeping warm

Arizonasaurus was a kind of crocodile.

It lived at the same time as the dinosaurs.

The **sail** on its back kept it warm.

It would turn around so the Sun was always shining on its sail.

Sun

Arizonasaurus
a-riz-o-na-sor-us

Sail

13

Little meat-eater

Eoraptor was one of the first **meat-eating dinosaurs**.

T. rex was a meat-eating dinosaur that lived many years after Eoraptor.
It had the same body shape but was much bigger!

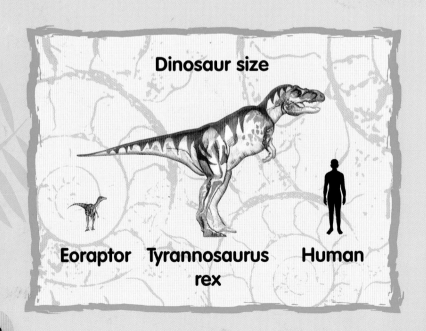

Dinosaur size

Eoraptor   Tyrannosaurus   Human
                 rex

Eoraptor was only one metre tall.

Eoraptor
ee-o-rap-tor

15

Unusual head

This dinosaur had a crest on top of its head.

Olorotitan
o-low-row-tie-tan

Dinosaur size

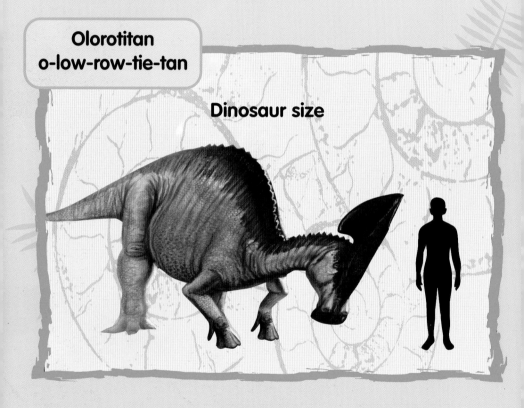

It might have used the crest to make a loud sound.

The crest was shaped like a fan.

16

Olorotitan was about nine metres long.

Crest

The pterosaurs

Pterosaurs lived at the same time as dinosaurs.

They did not have feathers but some were covered with hair.

Pterosaurs' wings were made of skin and **muscle**.

Tail

Wing

Pterosaur
terr-o-sor

19

Dinosaur in space

Coelophysis was a fast runner.

It ate small animals like lizards.

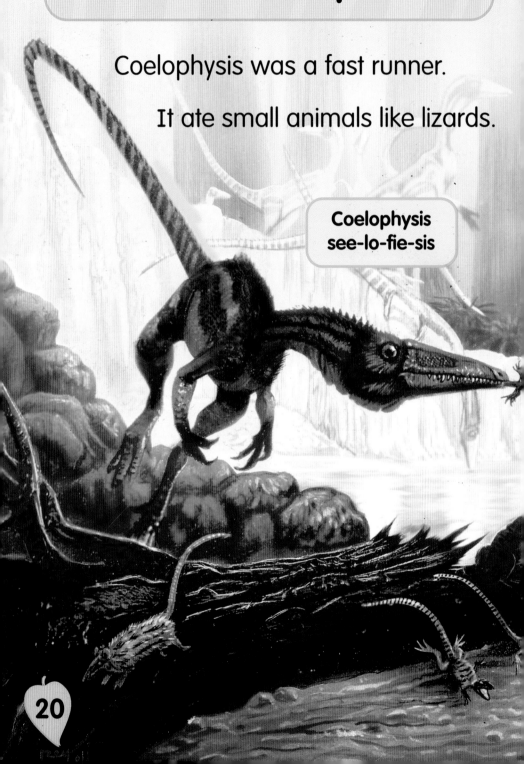

Coelophysis
see-lo-fie-sis

Astronauts took some Coelophysis bones on a **space shuttle**.

They thought it would be fun to take a dinosaur into space!

Glossary

meat-eating dinosaurs
Dinosaurs that ate other dinosaurs.

muscle
Soft parts of the body that allow movement or power.

pterosaurs
Flying animals that were living at the time of the dinosaurs.

sail
Long bones coming from the back and covered wth skin.

space shuttle
A manned space craft that can travel into space and back again.

Index

Copyright © ticktock Entertainment Ltd 2008
First published in Great Britain in 2008 by ticktock Media Ltd.,
Unit 2, Orchard Business Centre, North Farm Road, Tunbridge Wells, Kent TN2 3XF
ISBN 978 1 84696 764 1 pbk
Printed in China

We would like to thank: Penny Worms, Shirley Bickler, Suzanne Baker and the National Literacy Trust.

Picture credits (t=top, b=bottom, c=centre, l-left, r=right, OFC= outside front cover)
Lisa Alderson: 2, 9tl, 14bl, 15, 22t; John Alston: 14bc; Brian Edwards: 9bl, 10l, 10r, 22b; Natural History Museum: 5t, 7, 8; Luis Rey: 16-17, 20-21, 23b; Shutterstock: 4l, 4r, 5b, 6l, 6r, 9tr, 9br, 10 background; Chris Tomlin: 1, 12-13, 18-19, 23t; 23c.

Every effort has been made to trace the copyright holders, and we apologise in advance for any unintentional omissions. We would be pleased to insert the appropriate acknowledgements in any subsequent edition of this publication.

3 8002 01664 7374